KNOWING HIS BEST... WALKING IN REST!

**Trusting God For All He Is -
All He Has Said - All He Will Do**

Written and Compiled by Roy Lessin

Best Books

SILOAM SPRINGS, ARKANSAS

© Roy Lessin, Best to You Books, 1993.

All rights reserved. Written permission must be secured from the publisher to use or reproduce any part of this book, except for quotations in critical reviews or articles.

Published by

**Best to You,
Box 1300,
Siloam Springs, Arkansas 72761**

Scripture quotations are from The Holy Bible,
King James Version, and The Holy Bible,
New International Version (NIV),
Copyright © 1973, 1978, 1984 International Bible Society.
Used by permission of Zondervan Bible Publishers.
Printed in the United States.

There is a release, a freedom, a victory, a joy that can come
to us only when we have placed all that we are,
all that we have and all that we ever hope to be into the
caring hands of our heavenly Father. Once we have done
this, we need never doubt His ownership of us and His
purposes for us. We become persuaded that He is able to
keep all that we have committed to Him...confident that He
will do everything that is good and right concerning
us...assured that He guides us in perfect wisdom and total
love...certain that we can trust Him for all that is best.

"Come unto me all ye that labour and are heavy laden,
and I will give you rest. Take my yoke upon you,
and learn of me; for I am meek and lowly in heart:
and ye shall find rest unto your souls.
For my yoke is easy, and my burden is light."

Matthew 11: 28-30

KNOWING HIS BEST...

"...For I know whom I have believed,
and am persuaded that he is able to keep
that which I have committed
unto him against that day."

II Timothy 1:12

WALKING IN REST!

Truth brings rest to your soul.
In order to rest you need to be assured that your trust is in
someone and something that is certain and unchangeable.
Trust counts on God! He is pure;
there are no mixed motives in His heart...
He is the same; there is no variance in His nature...
He is faithful; there is no unreliability in His character.
He will never fail you, never let you down or cause you
to be ashamed. As you give yourself to Him,
you can live in the confidence of knowing that
your life couldn't be in better hands.

KNOWING
HIS BEST...

"And ye shall know the truth,
and the truth shall make you free."

John 8:32

WALKING IN REST!

Truth causes your heart to rest from anxiety,
worry and fear. Truth calms your spirit in troubled times
and brings your soul to quiet waters in the midst
of difficult times. Truth is the anchor that keeps you steady
and allows you to boldly sing, "It is well with my soul."
Truth lets you stand bravely...resist strongly...
fight confidently...conquer triumphantly.
Truth is the banner of your praise and
the confession of your faith
affirming that God has everything under control.

KNOWING HIS BEST...

"Behold, thou desirest truth in the inward parts:
and in the hidden part thou shalt
make me to know wisdom."

Psalm 51:6

WALKING IN REST!

Building truth within helps establish rest in the heart.
Lies are enemies that seek to bring confusion, distress, defeat
and unrest. Truth frees; lies bind...truth builds up;
lies tear down...truth nourishes;
lies poison...truth strengthens; lies weaken...truth quickens;
lies kill...truth heals; lies infect...truth restores;
lies rob...truth gladdens; lies depress...truth calms;
lies trouble...truth saves; lies condemn...truth lightens.
Truth renews the mind,
quickens the understanding
and takes every thought captive.

Knowing His Best...

"Whoever claims to live in him
must walk as Jesus did."

I John 2:6 NIV

WALKING IN REST!

Jesus was very busy. Each day was packed with people,
demands and ministry. He traveled; He taught; He preached.
Through and in it all He never panicked,
was never frustrated and never had a nervous breakdown.
He never cried out in despair, "I can't cope!"
It is His will for you to walk even as He walked.
He moved through each day in control...
functioned in peace...abode in rest.
He knew there was always enough time in each day
to do the Father's will.

Knowing
His Best...

"For it is God which worketh in you
both to will and to do of his good pleasure."

Philippians 2:13

WALKING IN REST!

Spiritual rest is the absence of self-generated action.
Spiritual rest lets God's will direct your motives and
His power direct your actions. Spiritual rest
frees you from the burden of pleasing others
to doing all to please Him. Spiritual rest moves you from
perplexity to divine purpose...
from over-loading to the Spirit's prompting...
from frustration to every good and perfect work.
Spiritual rest looks to God for guidance...
hears from God for approval...
waits on God for timing...
leans on God for sufficiency...
depends on God for results.

KNOWING HIS BEST...

"But by the grace of God I am what I am: and his grace
which was bestowed upon me was not in vain;
but I laboured more abundantly than they all:
yet not I, but the grace of God which was with me."

I Corinthians 15:10

WALKING IN REST!

God wants you to rest
not "from" the things He has for you
but "in" the things He has for you.
His rest reigns in the innermost part of your being.
It is deeper than temperament, personality or emotions...
it is not affected by job description,
education or environment...it flows
independent of possessions, comforts or conveniences.
Rest comes from grace...from the presence of the Lord...
from the comfort of the Holy Spirit...
from the yoke of Jesus Christ.

KNOWING
HIS BEST...

"For thus saith the Lord God, the Holy One of Israel;
In returning and rest shall ye be saved;
in quietness and in confidence shall be your strength...."

Isaiah 30:15

WALKING IN REST!

Rest is quiet trust. Quietness is freedom
from murmuring or complaint.
Quietness willingly yields to God's authority...
surrenders to the Lordship of Jesus Christ...
submits to the control of the Holy Spirit.
Quietness is a state of peace at heart and
personal well-being. It does the will of God
with an attitude of praise...a disposition of gratitude...
a makeup of joy. It is the assurance that you are
doing what God wants, in God's way,
at God's time, for God's glory.

KNOWING HIS BEST...

"The thief cometh not, but for to steal,
and to kill, and to destroy:
I am come that they might have life,
and that they might have it more abundantly."

John 10:10

WALKING IN REST!

The abundant life is knowing the best
that God has to give.
It is higher than your highest dreams...
deeper than your deepest desires...
greater than your greatest hopes.
You can be content because you know your life in Him
means you are not missing out on something better.
Your heart can rest because when you have found Him
to be your life, your search for meaning is over...
when you have heard His call,
your need for purpose has ended...
when you have followed His way,
your longing for direction has been fulfilled.

KNOWING HIS BEST...

"Who hath delivered us from the power of darkness, and hath translated us into the kingdom of his dear Son."

Colossians 1:13

WALKING IN REST!

Changing from turmoil to peace, from anxiety to trust,
from worry to assurance, from striving to rest
comes by changing kingdoms. God moves you from
a kingdom of darkness to a kingdom of light...
from a kingdom of selfishness to a kingdom of love...
from a kingdom of deception to a kingdom of truth.
It is a kingdom where the soul finds mercy
and the heart finds grace.
In His kingdom you are led, not driven...
guided, not pushed...healed, not tormented...
fulfilled, not frustrated...freed, not bound...
edified, not degraded...encouraged, not provoked...
released, not hindered.

KNOWING HIS BEST...

"That he would grant unto us, that we,
being delivered out of the hand of our enemies,
might serve him without fear."

Luke 1:74

WALKING IN REST!

God's work is to deliver you from every enemy of rest –
from fear that paralyzes, from worry that vexes,
from unbelief that despairs, from legalism that condemns.
His power overcomes weakness with strength,
mental anguish with a sound mind,
emotional distress with inner harmony,
spiritual bondage with freedom and praise.
His work will bring wholeness to your being...
healing to your body...
happiness to your heart.
He will take you from emptiness to fruitfulness
and from dead works to serve the living God.

KNOWING
HIS BEST...

"For where your treasure is,
there will your heart be also.
My heart is fixed, O God, my heart is fixed:
I will sing and give praise."

Matthew 6:21, Psalm 57:7

WALKING IN REST!

To be at rest, God must have your heart.
This means that He is at the very center of your being.
It means for you to live in Christ –
all that you have is yielded to Him,
all that you are is trusting in Him,
all that you ever hope to be is depending on Him.
He wants you to trust Him for your family,
for He has a Father's heart...trust Him for your health,
for He is the great physician...trust Him for your needs,
for He is your provider...trust Him with your life,
for He is the guardian and keeper of your soul.

KNOWING
HIS BEST...

"But godliness with contentment is great gain."

I Timothy 6:6

Walking in Rest!

Contentment is satisfaction with the place God has you
at the present. It is freedom from covetousness
and from the feeling of having to have "a little bit more" in
order to be happy. It delivers from greed and from the
stress that comes in trying to lay up treasures on earth.
Contentment says that God has been good to me...
that He will not fail me...that He knows what is best.
A contented life has learned to go without
instead of going into debt...has learned to wait
for God's time instead of moving in haste...
has learned to hold all things with
an open hand instead of a clenched fist.
Contentment seeks His kingdom first
and trusts God to add all that is needed.

KNOWING HIS BEST...

"I pray that out of his glorious riches
he may strengthen you with power through his Spirit
in your inner being."

Ephesians 3:16 NIV

Walking In Rest!

God wants to be glorified through all you do.
He wants you to approach each task
resting in the strength of His Spirit.
He wants you to enjoy inward harmony
as well as outward productivity.
Trust Him to bless the work of your hands
and to be the reward of your labors.
Your efforts will never go unnoticed...
your expectations will not be cut off...
nothing you do "as unto Him" will be wasted.

KNOWING
HIS BEST...

"Thy words were found, and I did eat them;
and thy word was unto me the joy
and rejoicing of mine heart:
for I am called by thy name, O Lord God of hosts."

Jeremiah 15:16

WALKING IN REST!

The sustenance for rest is the Word of God.
His word is more than history and information;
it is food. It is not only to be pondered and studied
but also to be eaten and digested.
His words are the only ones that can feed the spirit and
nurture the soul. They bring the manna of truth
to the mind and renew it in righteousness.
Through it the lies that bring unrest are defeated.
The Word assures you that life is not lived by chance or
luck but by the will and purposes of God
who sits on the throne of an unshakable and
unchanging kingdom. He will hold you steady;
He will keep you true.

KNOWING HIS BEST...

"For by grace are ye saved through faith;
and that not of yourselves: it is the gift of God:
Not of works, lest any man should boast."

Ephesians 2:8, 9

WALKING IN REST!

One of the greatest things that God delivers you from
is the struggle to save yourself.
Salvation is a work of rest.
It is a completed work; nothing needs to be added to it...
it is a total work; nothing needs to be done to improve it...
it is a final work; nothing needs to happen to change it.
The rest of salvation frees you from the bondage of trying
hard enough or being good enough to gain God's favor.
Resting in His finished work means receiving His salvation
as a free gift, given to you by His grace...
having a righteousness that is not your own,
given to you by Christ...
enjoying a new life that changes you,
brought to you by the presence of His Spirit.

Knowing His Best...

"Come unto me all ye that labour and are heavy laden, and I will give you rest."

Matthew 11:28

WALKING IN REST!

The reality of rest is found in the person of Jesus Christ.
He is at the center of every Christian experience
and everything that you have flows
out of your relationship with Him.
At the heart of your life in Him is not
a standard to live up to, a code to work out
or a list of regulations to follow.
Your life in Him is a walk with a friend
who sticks closer than a brother...
a fellowship of two spirits that are joined as one...
a union of hearts that are bonded together in love.

Knowing His Best...

"Do not be anxious about anything,
but in everything, by prayer and petition,
with thanksgiving, present your requests to God.
And the peace of God, which transcends all understanding,
will guard your hearts and your minds in Christ Jesus."

Philippians 4:6, 7 NIV

WALKING IN REST!

Rest comes through release.
Release is "placing" something into God's hands;
rest is "leaving" it in God's hands.
When something is released to God it is placed under
His authority and given to His control.
Release frees you from manipulation and from
the burden to have the final say.
Rest does not ignore personal responsibility
but it does release the weight of it.
Rest casts all cares on Him and
leaves all burdens at His feet.
Rest says, "God will sustain me"...
"The battle belongs to the Lord"...
"The Lord cares for me."

Knowing His Best...

"What is more, I consider everything a loss compared to the
surpassing greatness of knowing Christ Jesus my Lord,
for whose sake I have lost all things.
I consider them rubbish, that I may gain Christ."

Philippians 3:8 NIV

WALKING IN REST!

Rest comes through yielding.
When you release something to God
you place "it" in His hands, when you yield to God you
place "yourself" in His hands.
When you release something to God
you are giving Him your will;
when you yield to Him you are giving Him your heart.
A yielded heart lives for Him
and counts Him as the greatest one to know...
the highest goal to seek...the richest treasure to possess.
When the heart has the right motives,
when it seeks to gain Christ instead of personal reward,
when it seeks His approval instead of
the recognition of others, it can be at rest.

KNOWING
HIS BEST...

"But without faith it is impossible to please him:
for he that cometh to God must believe that he is,
and that he is a rewarder of them that diligently seek him."

Hebrews 11:6

Walking in Rest!

Rest means mixing everything with faith.
A will that releases all to God and a heart that yields all
to God can only do so with a faith that trusts all to God.
When faith is mixed with a released will, it can say,
"The Lord will do the right thing.
His grace does abound toward me.
I can do all things and face all things through Him.
The burden is the Lord's."
When mixed with a yielded heart, faith can say,
"He is the Lord of me and all I possess.
All I have is from Him
and for Him. I have no greater love
for I have Him."

KNOWING HIS BEST...

"Dear friends, if our hearts do not condemn us,
we have confidence before God
and receive from him anything we ask,
because we obey his commands and do what pleases him."

I John 3:21-22 NIV

Walking in Rest!

An obedient life is a life at rest.
Obedience keeps you from the many personal conflicts
that result from wanting and seeking your own way.
It keeps His peace in your heart,
His strength in your spirit and His balm upon your soul.
Obedience frees you from the need to defend your actions
and protect your image. An obedient life is at rest
because it knows that to obey is better than sacrifice...
that God's approval is more important than man's...
that the reward of the things gained far exceed
the loss of the things that have been given up.

KNOWING HIS BEST...

"Ye are of God, little children, and have overcome them:
because greater is he that is in you,
than he that is in the world."

I John 4:4

WALKING IN REST!

The great enemy of rest is the enemy of your soul.
He goes about as a roaring lion seeking to devour
your peace. His goal is to place heaviness upon you,
to accuse and falsely condemn you. He will challenge you
to doubt God and tempt you to do evil. He will lie to you
about God's character and your relationship to Him.
He will seek to confuse your thoughts and frustrate
your actions. The way to keep your rest against his assaults
is to expose his lies with truth...
to affirm your faith against his doubt...
to shine God's light upon his darkness...
to resist when he says yield...
say "thus it is written" when he says "has God said?"
You can rightly reject every thought that is not of
righteousness, peace or joy in your life.

KNOWING
HIS BEST...

"Thou hast given a banner to them that fear thee,
that it may be displayed because of the truth."

Psalm 60:4

Walking in Rest!

The triumph of rest within you can boldly wave
four banners of victory and praise:
"I fear not, for God is with me."
"I am still, for I know that He is God."
"I take no thought of tomorrow, for God goes before me."
"I am anxious for nothing,
for my life and times are in His hands."

KNOWING HIS BEST...

"For anyone who enters God's rest also rests
from his own work, just as God did his.
Now we who have believed enter that rest..."

Hebrews 4:10, 4:3 NIV

WALKING IN REST!

Faith is the embrace
that wraps its arms firmly around God's rest.
It is God's rest, not yours. Because God does not worry,
faith takes hold of God's peace...
because God does not fear, faith takes hold of God's power...
because God does not strive,
faith takes hold of God's authority.
Faith embraces the finished work of Christ's redemption...
the keeping work of the Holy Spirit...
the perfect work of the Father's will. Faith declares,
"God is my Father; He does all things well.
Jesus is my friend; He will never forsake me...
The Holy Spirit is my comforter;
He will never leave my side."

KNOWING HIS BEST...

"Keep your lives free from the love of money
and be content with what you have,
because God has said, "Never will I leave you;
never will I forsake you."

Hebrews 13:5 NIV

Walking in Rest!

Financial freedom brings great rest.
Financial freedom is not freedom from money but from
the love of it and the dependency upon it as a source of
security and happiness. Money can only find a proper place
in our lives when Christ has His proper place in our hearts.
The financially free heart has tasted of the Lord
and found Him to be good...
knows that it possesses the things that mean the most
and have the greatest worth...
believes that eternal things have the highest value.
It is a heart that has followed His ways
and found them true, trusted His word
and found Him faithful,
gazed upon His face
and found Him altogether lovely.

KNOWING HIS BEST...

"And having food and raiment [covering],
let us be therewith content."

I Timothy 6:8

Walking in Rest!

When our trust is in the Lord we will learn to be content
in whatever financial state He may have us.
Whether we are abounding with much or living on little,
the heart at rest never lets possessions possess it.
The heart at rest knows that no material possession
can add even one ounce of peace or joy to it.
It also knows that the absence of any material possession
cannot rob the heart of any of its peace or joy –
for the source of all inward peace and joy
is in the Holy Spirit.

KNOWING HIS BEST...

"Command those who are rich in this present world
not to be arrogant nor to put their hope in wealth,
which is so uncertain, but to put their hope in God,
who richly provides us with everything for our enjoyment."

I Timothy 6:17 NIV

WALKING IN REST!

Spiritual rest affects your entire makeup,
touching even your emotional and mental well-being.
Inner rest helps you relax and enjoy what you are doing
and the things around you. Rest brings a broader smile
to your face and a wider range to your laughter. The heart
at rest refreshes itself in the presence of the Lord...
rejoices in the goodness of the Lord...
delights in the ways of the Lord.
The heart at rest is not in turmoil during working times
nor condemned during leisure times.
It enjoys the Lord and the blessings He gives.
It knows that God is not stingy and
freely blesses His children with good things.

KNOWING HIS BEST...

"Thou hast turned for me my mourning into dancing:
thou hast put off my sackcloth,
and girded me with gladness."

Psalm 30:11

WALKING IN REST!

The heart at rest has cut the weights that keep
the joy of the Lord from welling up inside.
It is a heart that not only serves the Lord,
but serves Him with gladness...
that not only rejoices in good times,
but rejoices evermore...
that not only is grateful for some things,
but in everything gives thanks.
The closer the heart moves toward God
the deeper it moves in joy – it is the heart that is furthest
from Him that is the most miserable.
God is the Lord of happiness
and at His side are pleasures forevermore.

Knowing His Best...

"There remains, then, a Sabbath –
rest for the people of God."

Hebrews 4:9 NIV

WALKING IN REST!

At the heart of Biblical rest is the revelation of all that
God has done for you. On the seventh day God rested
because the work of creation was finished.
God didn't stop because the work was tiring
but because the work was complete.
As God rested from His work in creation,
so He wants you to rest in His work of redemption.
You enter the "Sabbath" of salvation –
a completed and finished work.
There is nothing you need to do
and nothing you need to add.
You need only to receive it, enjoy it and rest.

Knowing His Best...

"He hath made every thing beautiful in his time...."

Ecclesiastes 3:11

WALKING IN REST!

You can rest in knowing that He will make all things
beautiful as you wait for His time.
He does give the best to those who leave
the choice with Him. Never trust a timetable; trust God.
His timetable is different from ours.
Trusting means waiting on God and for God.
As you wait on God you are asking Him
to make you ready; as you wait for God
you are waiting until He is ready.
In His perfect way He will put together every detail...
arrange every circumstance...
change every heart and order every footstep
to bring to pass what He has for you.
He will never make a mistake.

KNOWING HIS BEST...

"Unto me, who am less than the least
of all saints, is this grace given,
that I should preach among the Gentiles
the unsearchable riches of Christ."

Ephesians 3:8

Walking In Rest!

Rest in the riches of all you have in Christ. Because you are in Him, you have received grace and gifts (Ephesians 4:7, 8), a hope laid up in heaven (Colossians 1:5), been made a partaker of the inheritance of the saints (Colossians 1:27), been delivered from the power of darkness (Colossians 1:13), been delivered from the wrath to come (I Thessalonians 1:10), received an everlasting consolation and good hope (II Thessalonians 2:16), been given the Spirit of power, love and a sound mind (II Timothy 1:7), His word effectively working in you (I Thessalonians 2:13), a crown of righteousness laid up for you (II Timothy 4:8), been given great and precious promises (II Peter 1:4), been given fellowship with the Father and His Son Jesus Christ (I John 1:3).

KNOWING
HIS BEST...

"Shew thy marvellous lovingkindness,
O thou that savest by thy right hand
them which put their trust in thee
from those that rise up against them."

Psalm 17:7

WALKING IN REST!

Rest sees things through God's eyes and weighs things
with His mind. The Lord wants you to stand in Him
and look around in confidence. He wants you to take
His point of view, for things are not always as they appear.
In the Lord you are not beneath things
to be pressed down and weighed in by them;
you are above things, seated with Him,
free from the defeat of all assaults, threats and accusations.
You are safe in the Lord as your tower...
strong in the Lord as your refuge...
protected in the Lord as your shield.
Flee to Him; His arms are open...hide in Him;
His wings will cover you...trust in Him;
His mighty arm will fight for you.

Knowing His Best...

"The eyes of your understanding being enlightened;
that ye may know what is the hope of his calling,
and what the riches of the glory
of his inheritance in the saints."

Ephesians 1:18

WALKING IN REST!

Rest in the riches of all you are in Christ. Because you are
in Him you are beloved of God (Romans 1:7),
justified freely by His grace (Romans 3:24), freed from sin
and alive unto God (Romans 6:7, 11), under grace
and a servant of righteousness (Romans 6:14, 18), married
to Christ (Romans 7:4), God's heir (Romans 8:16, 17),
free from the law of sin and death (Romans 8:1, 2),
a joint-heir with Christ and more than a conqueror
(Romans 8:17, 37), God's husbandry and His temple
(I Corinthians 3:9, 16), accepted in the beloved
(Ephesians 1:6), His workmanship (Ephesians 2:10),
a fellow citizen with the saints (Ephesians 2:19-20),
complete in Him (Colossians 2:10),
loved (II Thessalonians 2:16),
kept by His power (I Peter 2:10-11).

KNOWING
HIS BEST...

"But I have greater witness than that of John:
for the works which the Father hath given me to finish,
the same works that I do, bear witness of me,
that the Father hath sent me."

John 5:36

WALKING IN REST!

Rest is realizing the limits God has placed upon you.
He doesn't want you to do everything. He gives you
your assignments and enables you to do them.
Rest knows its place and is faithful in it.
Rest does not wish it had others' gifts or a different ministry.
Rest is content with what the Master gives.
Rest does not say "yes" to everything or run around
in circles trying to fulfill everyone's wishes and whims.
Rest quietly finds its place in God without being worn out
or stressed out with things that He has not ordered.

Knowing His Best...

"And God is able to make all grace abound toward you;
that ye, always having all sufficiency in all things,
may abound to every good work."

II Corinthians 9:8

Walking in Rest!

Rest finds its sufficiency in Christ.
Rest doesn't say, "I can do it."
It says, "God can do it through me."
In rest you never lean on your own understanding or
depend upon your own resources.
As you rest you are totally dependent on Him for all things
– you exchange your weakness for His strength...
your emptiness for His fullness...
your failure for His success...
your defeat for His victory...
your heaviness for His joy...
your uncleanness for His righteousness...
your restlessness for His peace.

Knowing His Best...

"Not that we are sufficient of ourselves
to think any thing as of ourselves;
but our sufficiency is of God."

II Corinthians 3:5

WALKING IN REST!

How blessed you are to find your sufficiency in God.
He is more than you have ever imagined
and greater than you have ever hoped He could be.
He will hear you when you call, teach you His ways,
guide you with His eye, show you His covenant,
give you certain victory, give you grace and glory,
lift up your head, be with you in trouble,
perfect that which concerns you,
fulfill the desires of your heart,
beautify you with salvation,
not withhold any good thing from you,
cause all things to work together for good.

Knowing His Best...

"In hope of eternal life,
which God, that cannot lie,
promised before the world began."

Titus 1:2

WALKING IN REST!

Your rest does not come by having faith in your faith,
your feelings, or your insights –
faith rests in the words of the One who cannot lie.
He does not need to tell you everything He is doing,
but He will tell you enough to keep you steady
and will reveal enough to give you hope.
There will always be a promise to claim...
there will always be a direction to follow...
there will always be a word to obey.
You will never be without a rock to stand upon...
you will never be without a foundation to build upon...
you will never be without a Savior to call upon.

Knowing
His Best...

"You will keep in perfect peace him whose mind is steadfast, because he trusts in you."

Isaiah 26:3 NIV

Walking in Rest!

The only reason to fear or worry is if the Lord had said:
1. Lay up treasures on earth
for there are no treasures in heaven.
2. Be anxious about life
for God doesn't know anything about you.
3. The most important thing in life is
what you possess, so get more.
4. Your Father doesn't care for you; you are on your own.
5. Seek what the world seeks; that is where true values are.
6. Be anxious about tomorrow;
it's good to have things pile up.
7. God cannot look after the practical details of life;
save yourself.

Knowing His Best...

"Blessed are the merciful: for they shall obtain mercy."

Matthew 5:7

WALKING IN REST!

God's rest within you will affect the relationships
around you. As you rest in His grace, mercy, forgiveness,
kindness and goodness, you will be able
to extend it to others. The blessing of rest in relationships
is in not demanding things from others
or constantly judging their performance.
It is a joy to be around those who give you the freedom
to be yourself and who won't reject you if you fail.
They accept you for who you are instead of trying to
change you...forgive you if you have offended...
extend love regardless of how you perform...
serve you instead of using you for selfish interests...
show you mercy instead of judgment for wrongs done.

Knowing His Best...

"For ye shall not go out with haste, nor go by flight:
for the Lord will go before you;
and the God of Israel will be your reward."

Isaiah 52:12

WALKING IN REST!

You can rest in knowing that God is always ahead
of you and always prepares things before He has you
walk in them. He made all things before He made you...
He loved you before you gave your heart to Him...
He came to you before you searched for Him...
He possessed all things before you had a need...
He knew all things before you had a question...
He finished His work of redemption
before He began His work in you...
He promised never to leave you
before He asked you to go...
He declared His victory before He asked you
to turn everything over to Him.

KNOWING
HIS BEST...

"Rest in the Lord, and wait patiently for him:
fret not thyself because of him who prospereth in his way,
because of the man who bringeth wicked devices to pass."

Psalm 37:7

WALKING IN REST!

"I wait on God to bring to pass all He has promised me,
and as I wait, I rest in faith in what I cannot see.
For in His way He will provide at just the perfect time
everything that's good and right to bless this life of mine."

KNOWING HIS BEST...

"I am the vine, ye are the branches.
He that abideth in me, and I in him,
the same bringeth forth much fruit:
for without me ye can do nothing."

John 15:5

WALKING IN REST!

To rest is to realize that God is your all in all.
Rest is never a 90 percent issue; it is always 100 percent.
The only thing you can do without God is fail.
The only way the Christian life is meant to be lived
is in total dependency upon Him.
Without Him no fruit remains, no gifts abide,
no hope prevails, no strength endures,
no love conquers, no faith overcomes.

Knowing His Best...

"O LORD, you have searched me and you know me."

Psalm 139:1 NIV

Walking in Rest!

You can rest in the Lord because He knows you
better than anyone else (You discern my lying down;
You are familiar with all my ways.), understands you more
than anyone else (Before a word is on my tongue,
You know it completely.), cares for you more than
anyone else (You have laid Your hand upon me.),
is nearer than anyone else (If I go to the heavens,
You are there. If I make my bed in the depths,
You are there...Your hand will guide me,
Your right hand will hold me fast.), watches over you closer
than anyone else (You created my inmost being:
You knit me together in my mother's womb.),
loves you more than anyone else
(How precious to me are Your thoughts, O God.
How vast is the sum of them.).

KNOWING
HIS BEST...

"For of him, and through him, and to him,
are all things: to whom be glory for ever. Amen."

Romans 11:36

Walking in Rest!

Rest is trusting God for everything and in everything.
He is rest to your ears,
for He speaks in a still small voice...
your eating, for He will bless your food and water...
your body, for He is your health...
your labors, for He will reward you...
your family, for He will build your house...
your children, for they will be taught of the Lord...
your trials, for He will not allow you to go through
more than you can bear...
your decisions, for He will guide you with His eye...
your future, for He prepares the way before you.

Knowing His Best...

"...All my springs are in thee."

Psalm 87:7

Walking in Rest!

He is big enough, strong enough, wise enough,
powerful enough and caring enough
to see you through every circumstance of life.
You are not alone in anything you face.
You are His child;
never act or think like an orphan.

Knowing His Best...

"Many are the woes of the wicked,
but the LORD's unfailing love
surrounds the man who trusts in him."

Psalm 32:10 NIV

Walking in Rest!

"I have the wisdom and the resources to take care
of every detail of your life.
It is My responsibility and delight to provide for you.
I see what is ahead. I direct the steps you are taking.
To worry is to question Me.
To strive is to be unsure of My power.
To fear is to doubt My love. I care about you. I love you.
You are mine. I will never forget about you.
Don't carry burdens I do not want you to bear. Be done
with anxiety. It is not fitting for you.
Let My words heal you. Let Me release you from the weight
you carry. Give all your cares to Me. My hand is over you;
My grace upon you. You shall not want any good thing."
Lovingly,
Your Father.

Knowing His Best...

"Let the morning bring me word of your unfailing love,
for I have put my trust in you.
Show me the way I should go,
for to you I lift up my soul."

Psalm 143:8 NIV

WALKING IN REST!

Rest in your relationships, your work, your decisions,
your daily walk. Rest in your mind, your spirit,
your emotions. Rest in the future, the day, the moment.
Trust Him. Rest in your salvation, your blessings, your gifts.
Rest in His presence, His purpose, His plans.
Begin each day in the joy of forgiveness,
the power of the Holy Spirit and the hope of eternal life.
Affirm that He is looking after you
and has not forgotten you.
Trust Him for the details of each day.
Be at rest as you drive, as you shop,
as you labor, as you play.
Let His calm soothe you, His balm heal you,
His stillness quiet you.
Know His best and walk in rest.

Be assured that regardless
of where you are,
what you are doing,
or what you're going through...
In all things, in all ways,
God is doing the most
loving thing concerning you!